RUSSIAN BALLET
ON TOUR

RUSSIAN BALLET
ON TOUR

Alexander Orloff

Margaret E. Willis

RIZZOLI
NEW YORK

To my parents
for their contribution and life-long dedication to this art

This edition first published 1989 by
Rizzoli International Publications Inc.,
300 Park Avenue South,
New York,
NY 10010

Book concept by Alexander Orloff
Photographs © 1989 by Alexander Orloff
Text © 1989 by John Calmann and King Ltd

Library of Congress Cataloging-in-Publication Data
Orloff, Alexander.
Russian ballet on tour/photographs by Alexander Orloff,
text by Margaret Willis.
p.   cm.
Includes index.
ISBN 0–8478–1106–9
1. Ballet companies—Russian S.F.S.R.   2. Ballet companies—
Russian S.F.S.R.—History.   3. Ballet companies—Russian S.F.S.R.—
Pictorial works.   I. Willis, Margaret.   II. Title.
GV1785.8.075   1989
792.8′0947—dc20
89–42793
CIP

This book was designed and produced by
JOHN CALMANN AND KING LTD, LONDON

Designed by Behram Kapadia
Typeset by Fakenham Photosetting Ltd, Fakenham, Norfolk
Printed in Singapore by Toppan Ltd

Contents

Introduction

The Russian ballet on tour—the idea fires the imagination of every balletomane. For a thousand years, the name 'Russia' has conjured up vast regions of ice and snow or expanses of desolate steppe—a land whose bleak remoteness isolated its peasantry from contact with the rest of Europe. After World War II, Stalin's Iron Curtain sealed it off even more effectively. At Stalin's death, Khrushchev launched a process of 'thaw', and in 1956 Russian ballet dancers suddenly burst onto a western stage—that of the Royal Opera House at Covent Garden in London. Overnight, a new image of Russia was forged: fire rather than ice. Here were superbly trained, refined, dramatic artists, heirs to a tradition that stretched back more than two centuries. Their disciplined technique, combined with their emotional and expressive eloquence, dazzled western audiences and critics.

That first full-fledged tour was by the Bolshoi Company of Moscow. The Kirov's initial tour to Paris, London and New York came in 1961. Almost three decades later, Russian dancers still fascinate and impress the outside world, although they are considerably less mysterious now. The Bolshoi, the Kirov of Leningrad, the Moscow Classical Ballet and individual stars such as Maya Plisetskaya and Vladimir Vasiliev tour more than ever before. Their names and their art are known from Europe to the United States, from Japan to Mexico, from Brazil to Australia, from Syria to Havana. In the new spirit prompted by Mikhail Gorbachev's *glasnost*, the travel looks set to continue. Communist leaders are happy to finance this continuation of Czarist tradition, out of pride in their country's achievements and in the knowledge that the Soviet Union of today has no better ambassador than the heirs of the Russian ballet of yesterday.

The photographs in this book capture the drama, the movement and the grace of the Russian ballet on tour. Dancers are shown in performance, in rehearsal, in daily class at the barre. They range from established stars to young hopefuls shown at home in the Vaganova School of the Kirov Company in Leningrad, striving to attain the standards that will enable them to join any company in the Soviet Union, and ultimately to grasp one of the greatest prizes and privileges in a closed society—travel abroad.

The companies photographed range from the Kirov and Bolshoi, each with more than two hundred years of history behind them, to the twenty-three-year-old Moscow Classical Ballet. The photographs are a chronicle of balletic achievement, an historical record of a decade of Russian tours, and a catalogue of the choreographic art.

(*Opposite*) Preparing for class at the Vaganova School, Leningrad.

The Vaganova All-Russia Ballet Competition, inaugurated in 1988 to mark the 250th anniversary of the founding of the original school. The boys' *barre* exercises.

The early tours profoundly influenced ballet in the West. The Russians presented an art form that reached past the exclusive, purist domain of classical ballet to the edge of popular entertainment, something to be enjoyed by a mass audience. Russian ballet was alive. Its dancers reached every part of the stage, sweeping it with big, space-consuming movements. They soared into the air and turned like tops, their speed of movement was astonishing; yet they never let go of their classic inheritance— firm, strongly arched backs, fluid arms whose movements stretched out to the tips of the fingers, and soft landings in perfect positions.

The *corps de ballet* of both companies showed hitherto unattained levels of precision and harmony. The greatest impact, though, was a change in the way that the male dancer was perceived. No longer was he merely the subordinate partner, but an equal with the ballerina. The virile virtuosity of dancers such as Vasiliev scotched the widespread notion of male dancers as weak and effeminate. But the ballerinas, too, surpassed expectations. Dancers such as Plisetskaya and Struchkova electrified their audiences. Above all, Galina Ulanova was an inspiration to the western ballet world. A supremely lyrical ballerina in the finest technical tradition, she had the ability to move audiences to tears with her interpretations.

Western critics are quick to point out that massive state financial support allowed the big Bolshoi and Kirov companies to choose only the best dancers to come on tour. But the Russians' best has generally been on a different plane from anything seen in the West.

Members of the Kirov company at class. The teacher is Ninel Kurgapkina.

The Russians on tour have not only affected the West; the West has in some ways affected them. On one level, dancers have had an opportunity to view capitalism at first hand, and to take home the consumer goods it has to offer. On the artistic side, they are interested in the much wider range of western choreography, and in the greater freedom western dancers have had to develop their own careers. In Russia, dancers are, in effect, at the mercy of company leaders.

In 1961 Rudolf Nureyev caused world headlines by defecting from a Kirov tour in Paris; in 1970 Natalya Makarova defected from the Kirov in London; in 1974, Mikhail Baryshnikov, also of the Kirov, left a Soviet dance tour in Canada. These three extraordinary dancers have inspired and revitalized the spirit of many companies and dancers around the world. Their careers have developed myriad facets of their superb training. Their contributions to western ballet history cannot be measured. For years after their defections, they were 'non-persons' at home, written out of Kirov history. It was not until 1988 that a combination of *glasnost* and the 250th anniversary of the Kirov's ballet school, where all were trained, led to their reinstatement in the USSR. In a corner of the Vaganova Museum, where the costume worn by Nijinsky in *Spectre de la Rose* hangs, and a pair of Anna Pavlova's dancing shoes is enshrined in a glass case, is now a modest photo collection of all three dancers: nothing special, just one set of black and white photos among many others.

Also in 1988, Nureyev was allowed back into the Soviet Union to visit his ailing mother. In March, Baryshnikov appeared in a gala honouring Maya Plisetskaya in the USA, and took classes with the

Bolshoi Company. In August, Makarova was granted permission to perform with the Kirov on its London tour, and in January 1989 she was allowed back to Leningrad to dance once again with the Kirov Company where she began her career thirty years ago—a highly emotional occasion.

The first Bolshoi defections came on the 1979 tour of the United States: first with Alexander Godunov, in New York, followed a few weeks later by Valentina and Leonid Kozlov in Los Angeles. Tours to the US and the UK were halted, though Russians kept visiting other areas of the world. The Bolshoi returned to London in 1986 for the first time in 12 years, and to the US in 1987 after eight years. Meanwhile both companies could regularly be seen in Italy and Paris, though the Kirov did not return to the United States until 1986 (a gap of 22 years) and to Britain until 1988 (after 17 years). A whole generation of its dancers had come and gone in the meantime.

The artistry that the Russians bring on tour, carefully polished and preserved over two centuries, was originally imported from Europe. The roots of Russian ballet grew out of French soil.

Late in the seventeenth century, Czar Peter the Great opened up his country in an attempt to draw it closer to the progressive, prosperous way of life in Europe. By early in the eighteenth century everything with a 'foreign' label was considered fashionable and desirable; at the Russian court it was the French style that was adopted and copied, from costume to language. In his travels, Peter had been impressed by the elegant social life of Europe; on his return he took pleasure in hosting masquerades and balls. He elevated the status of dance, which until then had been considered only as a low form of entertainment. It was used as padding for the plentiful and popular opera productions of the time, and tolerated, though not necessarily enjoyed, by theatre audiences.

In 1734, a young French ballet-master by the name of Jean-Baptiste Landé was invited to the Czarist capital of St Petersburg to train military cadets in formal dancing. Two years later, his success was evident when more than one hundred of the boys danced professionally in an opera at the Court. In 1738, Landé was given permission to open a ballet school in the Winter Palace for the children of palace servants. He received support and encouragement in his work, first from the Empress Anna, and later from Peter's daughter, the Empress Elizabeth. Here, at the first ballet school in Russia, 12 girls and 12 boys learned their intricate lessons quickly and were soon appearing in Court productions. Thus Landé formed the foundation of a professional ballet theatre in Russia and the training-ground for its own style of classical ballet. The traditions are strictly adhered to and have been devotedly passed down through the years by generations of teachers and performers.

The aristocracy of St Petersburg loved this new expression of foreign culture, which continued under the tutelage of the Austrian Frantz Hilferding and later his Italian pupil Gasparo Angiolini. The latter was specifically invited by Catherine the Great, whose support for dance led to a decree that the professional ballet theatre should be secured under State sponsorship.

When news of the French Revolution of 1789 reached the capital, there was great fear of political contamination. Artists and works from what was now considered enemy territory were banned for the duration of the unrest in France. The removal of French influence from the ballet scene actually benefited the development of Russia's own national style of classical dance; it was during this time that the Moscow-born Ivan Valberkh, a graduate of the Petersburg Ballet School, became the first Russian ballet-master. He also produced several notable patriotic ballets, especially during the Napoleonic invasion of 1812. His ballet *Love for the Motherland* so aroused the audience's patriotism that, it is said, many went straight from the theatre to enlist in the army.

(*Opposite*) A Kirov class given by Ninel Kurgapkina during the company's Paris tour:
(*facing*) Marat Daukayev, Faroukh Ruzimatov.

Members of the Bolshoi company at class: Alexander Vetrov (*foreground*).

Folk-dancing was very much part of the heritage of ancient Rus. The first references to *khorovod* (circle) and *prisiadka* (knee squatting) dances were recorded in the sixth century. These peasant displays, performed at festivals and celebrations, were full of action, movement and the Russian *dysha*, or soul. A German scientist visiting Russia in the late 1770s reported that he found the national dance style eloquent and beautiful not only for the intricacies of the steps but also for the way in which the dancers moved every part of their bodies. The Russian style of ballet began to develop: the classical training was stamped with these lively folk elements and imbued with great powers of expression. From this combination of European foundations and Russian character emerged a unique artistic form.

Meanwhile, more indigenous ideas were flowering to the south, in Moscow. In 1764, the Moscow Orphanage was founded on the banks of the Moskva River. As its young wards grew up, they were taught dancing along with acting, crafts and sciences. In 1773, an Italian teacher, Filippo Beccari, was engaged to turn these young people into professional dancers. Given a mere three years to do it, he nonetheless decided to accept the payment of 250 roubles per pupil only for those who succeeded in making the grade. Of his class of 62, 26 became fully fledged soloists. Beccari made the tidy sum of 6,500 roubles and the foundations were laid in Moscow of what was later to be known as the Bolshoi Ballet School.

Just as the architectural characters of the two cities were very different—St Petersburg formally planned and laid out in classical straight lines at the end of the seventeenth century, Moscow a maze of medieval streets and a jumble of building styles radiating from the central fortress of the Kremlin—so the arts of the cities differed as well. In St Petersburg, Court circles were mannered and conservative, but in the bustling, cosmopolitan trading-centre that was Moscow, the atmosphere was freer. As the intellectual centre of the country, Moscow demanded dramatic realism on its stage. Although Moscow University boasted two theatre schools, most of the city's theatres were privately owned, allowing more freedom of choice and individuality in productions. In this atmosphere, Moscow developed a different style of dance to appeal to an audience different from that of St Petersburg. The separate styles of the Bolshoi and the Kirov are still apparent today.

On to the Moscow scene now came an Englishman, Michael Maddox. Maddox was an engineer, in Moscow to demonstrate various mechanical and theatrical gadgets. He joined forces with Prince Urusov, a patron of the arts, and the two were granted a government licence to promote ballet in the capital. In 1776, the first ballets were performed by dancers from the Moscow Orphanage in the Znamensky Opera House, near the site of today's Bolshoi Theatre.

In St Petersburg, European influences remained strong. Many of Europe's internationally renowned dancers and teachers continued to flock there. After the French Revolution came Charles-Louis Didelot, renowned for flying across the stages of London on wires. He came to Russia expecting to find little culture, but was surprised to discover both strong theatrical traditions and a well-established style of ballet, thanks to the early work of Valberkh. In the 1820s Didelot introduced the Russians to a more graceful way of dancing by changing the style of the costumes: instead of the outfits of heavy conventional material, he often dressed his dancers in sleeveless tunics of gauze. He put the leading ballerinas up on pointe, creating an impression of flight. The age of the Romantic ballet had arrived.

The most famous exponent of pointe-work in the 1830s was Maria Taglioni, a Swedish-Italian dancer who came to St Petersburg after triumphing in Europe. Though not the first to dance on pointe, she raised the standard of dancing on the tips of the toes from a virtuoso stunt into an expression of artistry. Russian audiences loved Taglioni, seeing in her the ideal of the Romantic dancer. She expressed both purity and buoyancy in ballets choreographed by her father Filippo Taglioni, especially in *La Sylphide*.

The Romantic era continued to flourish under the guidance of the choreographer Jules Perrot, who arrived in St Petersburg from France in 1848. He brought with him several of his masterpieces, including the greatest Romantic ballet of all, *Giselle*, which he had jointly created with Jean Coralli. The original ballet opened in Paris in 1841; it disappeared from European repertoires in 1868, but, happily, was preserved in Russia where it became a classic. It was re-introduced to the West in 1911 by the Diaghilev company. Perrot, much-loved and respected, was succeeded by Arthur Saint-Léon, whose contract with the Imperial Theatre stipulated that he not only mount and revive large numbers of ballets, but dance and play the violin as well.

Despite the domination of these Italian and French choreographers and teachers, a Russian-ness of style continued to grow in both St Petersburg and Moscow. Productions of the 1860s and 1870s lacked originality and interest, so a search began for more creative works. It turned up just two, but these were enough to inspire and to find a lasting place in the repertory: Saint-Léon's *Koniok Gorbunok* ('The Little Hump-backed Horse'), first performed in St Petersburg in 1864, and Petipa's lively, bustling *Don Quixote*, produced in Moscow in 1869 on orders of the Directorate of the Imperial Theatres—and taken to St Petersburg two years later in a more academic and subdued version.

It was the Frenchman Marius Petipa who brought the art of Russian ballet to its apex. He moulded and blended the technical qualities of the dancers with the works which best presented them. Despite never learning the language (he lived in Russia for 63 years), Petipa nonetheless absorbed the Russian culture and created balletic works that remain favourites today: *La Bayadère* (first produced in 1877 at the Maryinsky Theatre in St Petersburg); *Sleeping Beauty*, and *Swan Lake*.

At the end of the nineteenth century, when dance in Europe was beginning to decline, ballet in Russia kept a firm hold of its classical foundations. Yet there were challenges. The dancers in St

Petersburg lacked artistic guidance and began searching for new kinds of balletic expressions—new trends and new productions. The ballet establishment in St Petersburg remained conservative, and frowned on innovation. Tension grew. On the stage productions radiated glitter. Backstage it was another picture: poor working conditions, undercurrents of dissatisfaction and resentment at injustice as a general political unrest stirred throughout the country. The dancers had been cocooned in their own private world since childhood. Now many became involved in the developments outside, and claimed the right to fight for artistic freedom. Revolutionary meetings and a strike resulted—an atmosphere not wholly conducive, it might seem, to the flowering of artistic talent.

Yet in those final days of the old order, before 1917, arose a galaxy of brilliant stars whose collective talents have never been surpassed. They were to win recognition for themselves and fame for the name of Russian ballet around the world. Products of the Imperial School, they brought outstanding artistry, lyricism and vitality, the very essence of the Russian classical heritage, on to the stage of St Petersburg's Maryinsky Theatre. Among them were Anna Pavlova, the daughter of a Petersburg laundress, who was to become the most famous ballerina the world has ever known; Vaslav Nijinsky, whose elevation and technical virtuosity became legendary; Tamara Karsavina, an ethereal, classical ballerina of the greatest expressivity; and Michel Fokine, a dancer of exceptional talent and a choreographer of integrity who, dissatisfied with the expressionless ballets of his day, and recognizing the need for reforms, created such enduring works as *The Dying Swan*, *Petrushka*, *Schéhérazade*, *The Firebird*, *Le Spectre de la Rose* and *Chopiniana* (*Les Sylphides*).

Into the spotlight at this period came a young man called Serge Diaghilev, co-founder of the art magazine *Mir Iskusstva* ('The World of Art'), editor of the Annual of the Imperial Theatres, and artistic adviser to the Maryinsky. Diaghilev organized cultural 'Russian Seasons' in Paris, and in 1909 was given permission to present a troupe of dancers. This was the first time the Russian ballet had been seen abroad. It had a rapturous reception.

Diaghilev's 'Ballets Russes' company illuminated the stages of Paris and London with grandeur, colour and excitement; it rekindled balletic inspiration in Europe, and especially in France. Now the West was taking the best of Russian style and building on it, while this very style, so long dynamic, was beginning to lose momentum at home. In trying to preserve the purity and form of its tradition, Russians, suspicious of change, were stifling it.

The dancers found this stagnation when they returned home after tours. To continue progressing, many dancers (and other Russian artists) felt compelled to leave their homeland for the West, where the atmosphere was less restricting.

During these years the focus of the Russian ballet world had been slowly shifting from St Petersburg to Moscow. In 1898 the Bolshoi found itself on the threshold of a new episode in its history when Alexander Gorsky came to mount *Sleeping Beauty*. Trained in St Petersburg, Gorsky was impressed by the intellectual and expressive atmosphere of Moscow and readily accepted the opportunity to work there as *régisseur* (artistic director). Gorsky's vision was to help lead the Bolshoi Company away from the aesthetic, refined productions of the Maryinsky along a more flamboyant path. Dramatic action went hand in hand with virtuoso technique. Among the many ballets he revised was Petipa's *Don Quixote*. His was a bold, dramatic version, filled with Spanish elements in both décor and choreography. It is still danced at the Bolshoi today.

Ballet itself was threatened by the upheavals that culminated in the revolution of 1917. To the Bolsheviks, ballet seemed a throwback to Czarist privilege, an entertainment for the aristocracy. A saviour appeared in the unlikely form of Lenin's first Minister for Education, Anatoli Lunarcharsky, who happened to be an admirer of ballet. In a passionate speech from the Bolshoi stage itself, he suggested that the art could be a useful propaganda tool in educating the people to the new ways of the Soviet republic. He hailed ballet as 'the foundation of a new artistic culture . . . belonging to the people'. His efforts did indeed save the old artistic culture of Russian ballet.

The Maryinsky Theatre in Leningrad, the home of the Kirov.

In 1918 Lenin moved the capital of the newly-created USSR from St Petersburg to Moscow. The Bolshoi School was taken over for use as a military hospital. The theatre, difficult to heat in a time of shortages, was constantly threatened with closure. On each occasion Lenin himself stepped in to keep it open.

Theatres now filled with a different kind of audience. For the first time, with tickets freely available, the doors of the Kirov and the Bolshoi opened to factory workers, peasants and soldiers.

There was much pressure from the revolutionary leaders to find innovative and experimental art forms for the new era. Since the cream of Russian choreographers, dancers and ballet-masters had by now fled from the revolution, there was also a pressing need to find teachers who were capable of continuing the Russian heritage and combining it with a new, Soviet, style. In St Petersburg, now renamed Petrograd, a small energetic woman, the daughter of a box-office attendant at the Maryinsky Theatre and a dancer with the company for 22 years, stepped into the breach. Agrippina Vaganova took up teaching in 1919 and in the following years not only taught such stars as Semyonova, Ulanova, Dudinskaya and Kolpakova, but carefully developed a teaching method that was to inspire and guide ballet-dancers for generations. Today the ballet school in Leningrad is named after her; her teaching techniques form the foundation of all Soviet ballet schools and are widely used throughout the world.

At the Bolshoi, the dancers retained some of the old classical ballets, though Gorsky experimented with them, even changing stories or traditional effects. In his 1920 version of *Swan Lake*, the swans

The Vaganova School: class taken by Natalia Dudinskaya. The pupils are Nastia Dunetz and
Alla Dimitrieyeva. The portrait is that of Agrippina Vaganova, the school's founder.

wore loose-fitting tunics rather than traditional tutus. The company also began to appear in works with
frankly political subjects such as the one-act ballet *Stenka Rasin*, created by Gorsky for the first
anniversary of the revolution. Here the theme was not of fairytale princes and princesses but of real-life
people protesting against tyranny. Kasyan Goleizovsky offered impressionistic, logically planned yet
often controversial works, which broke away from a classical base. (His work had a strong influence on
a young Georgian dancer in Leningrad named Georgi Balanchivadze—later George Balanchine.) In
1927, Vasili Tikhomirov created *The Red Poppy*, a heroic ballet about a beautiful Chinese girl who
gives her life to save Soviet soldiers.

Meanwhile, in Petrograd, now called Leningrad, the Company of the State Academic Theatre of
Opera and Dance (the former Maryinsky; it would not take the name Kirov until 1935) was led through
the post-revolutionary years by Fyodor Lopukhov, an outstanding character dancer and choreographer. Against strong opposition, he managed to preserve much of the classical repertoire while also
creating new forms of dance expression.

In 1922, Lopukhov choreographed the first plotless symphonic-style ballet, *Dance Symphony*, to
Beethoven's Fourth Symphony. One of its dancers was the 19-year-old Balanchine, who was soon to
leave Russia to join Diaghilev's company. Developing the principles of this style of classical ballet,
Balanchine moulded and expanded them into a unique neoclassical style which today directly links the
New York City Ballet, which he founded, with the Russian traditions.

As the 1930s began, dancers and ideas flowed back and forth between Leningrad and Moscow.
Choreography, influenced by the Stanislavsky acting method, became more dramatic and ideological.

The orchestra pit at the Bolshoi Theatre. The conductor is Algis Zhuraitis.

Ballets such as Vasily Vainonen's *Flames of Paris*, set in the French Revolution, and Vakhtang Chaboukiani's *Laurencia*, about peasant uprisings in Spain, demanded new types of powerful, virtuoso dancers. Alongside these nationalistic productions, the traditional ballets and new non-political works continued to appear. Literary classics such as Pushkin's *The Fountain of Bakhchisarai* and *The Prisoner of the Caucasus*, Gogol's *Taras Bulba*, and Shakespeare's *Romeo and Juliet* required more characterization and realism. Into this era stepped an unassuming ballerina called Galina Ulanova, who was destined to become a legend in her own time. Trained at the Theatre School under Vaganova, she joined the Kirov Company in 1928, making her début as Princess Florine in *Sleeping Beauty*. She was quickly noticed for her expressive, lyrical quality. On stage, Ulanova came alive. Taking on the identity of her role strongly and sensitively, she transcended the limits of actress and dancer and *became* Juliet or Giselle for the duration of the performance. When she began to travel overseas in the late 1940s, Ulanova shone as the diamond in the crown of Russian ballet, blending old-world ballet traditions with Soviet drama and characterization.

During the Great Patriotic War (as the Russians call World War II) the bulk of both companies had been evacuated to avoid the Nazi advance, though theatres stayed open and some performances continued. The Bolshoi went east to Kuibyshev on the River Volga; the Kirov escaped from Leningrad before Hitler besieged the city for 900 days, and went north-east to Perm. Despite difficult living and working conditions, the two companies were able to produce new works, keeping ballet traditions alive.

After World War II, with the government established in the Kremlin, the focus of Soviet ballet was now definitively centred on the Bolshoi, which performed for state officials and visitors and national congresses. Several of the great dancers, including Ulanova, moved down from Leningrad with successful productions, stocking the Bolshoi Company with a wealth of Kirov talent.

The bleak post-war years saw many more hardships, yet from them budded artistic talent. At the Bolshoi, two Prokofiev ballets were among the most popular: *Cinderella*, choreographed by Rotislav Zakharov, showed the sparkling Olga Lepeshinskaya in the title role, while Leonid Lavrovsky's powerful *Romeo and Juliet* was revived with Ulanova again receiving ovations for her sensitive Juliet.

At the Kirov, Konstantin Sergeyev and Natalia Dudinskaya continued to present the finest classical techniques, as did Alla Osipenko, Yuri Soloviev, and Irina Kolpakova, Vaganova's last pupil.

Following the pioneering trail blazed by Lopukhov, new choreographers began to search for contemporary themes at the Kirov. In 1961, Igor Belsky recalled the war years in his dramatic *Leningrad Symphony* to Shostakovich's Seventh Symphony, with Alla Sizova and Yuri Soloviev in the leading roles; Leonid Yacobsen created his version of Khachaturian's *Spartacus*, done on demi-pointe and in stylistic poses; Yuri Grigorovich produced Prokofiev's *Stone Flower* in 1957, putting emphasis on the role of the *corps* and including athletic movement based on folk-dance. In 1968, two Bolshoi dancers, Natalia Kasatkina and Vladimir Vasiliov (not to be confused with the great dancer Vasiliev), created a gymnastic, comical version of the Adam and Eve story in *Creation of the World* for a young dancer in the Kirov called Mikhail Baryshnikov. Konstantin Sergeyev, the *danseur noble* and partner of Ulanova, and director of the company, 1951–55 and 1960–70, choreographed several ballets, including a clear, concise version of *Hamlet*, to music by Nikolai Chervinsky.

The Kirov company seen by western audiences today has, since 1977, been shaped by Oleg Vinogradov. After training at the Vaganova School, Vinogradov went east to join the company in the Siberian city of Novosibirsk. There, in 1964, he staged a new production of *Cinderella*, and in 1965, *Romeo and Juliet*. The originality of the ballets—continuous dancing instead of mime scenes in *Cinderella*, for instance—aroused much interest and he was invited to create works for other companies, including the Bolshoi. After five years as director of the Maly Theatre in Leningrad, Vinogradov took vigorous command of the Kirov. He changed the entire *corps de ballet*, insisting that all members must be of uniform size, and of attractive appearance; he retired older dancers; he brought in ballerinas from Perm; he changed staff and *régisseurs*. Today he has plans to increase the 218-member company by 100, and to put dancers on contract, encouraging more competition and participation. At present, dancers draw salaries whether they dance or not. The new plan would be to have a basic salary, augmented by extra fees for each performance.

Vinogradov's participation in the daily workings of the Kirov Ballet is tireless. He keeps a close eye on company standards, dropping in unexpectedly to daily classes and rehearsals, and attending each performance, sitting in a box by the stage or, more often, in Row 17 to get a straight-on view. During intervals he goes back-stage to make comments to the dancers; at the end of each performance, the production staff (including the ballet coaches) go to his office on the fourth floor for a post-mortem conference.

The Kirov Ballet of today preserves many of the old ballets in its repertoire while adding new works. Vinogradov himself has touched up several of the old masterpieces, restoring them yet leaving their original balletic tapestry intact. In 1986, he restored in full the Petipa ballet *Le Corsaire*, an adventure story of shipwrecks, pirates, slave-markets and oriental mystique, set in a classical framework. Its success is partly due to the vivid set designs of Teimuraz Murvanidze, whose 'Jardin Animé' comes complete with splashing fountains. The restoration of such a piece of balletic history is important: it shows the intricate *enchaînements* and individual variations common to ballet productions of the middle of the nineteenth century, when *Le Corsaire* was created.

Another success has been the full-length production of *La Bayadère*. Set in ancient India, it tells of the love between Nikia, a young temple dancer, or bayadère, and Solor, a warrior. When Nikia is killed the heartbroken Solor dreams of meeting her again in the Kingdom of the Shades. It is at the beginning of this scene that the famous procession of Bayadères is to be seen, and here the flawless timing and

Konstantin Zaklinsky and Olga Chenchikova of the Kirov rehearsing LA BAYADÈRE in the
Maryinsky Theatre.

discipline of the Kirov *corps de ballet* is unsurpassed. *Paquita*, which is set in Spain, depicts a French
officer in love with a Spanish gipsy girl. The variations and Grand Pas of Act III are a showcase in
which the individual dancers can sparkle.

Vinogradov has chosen varied subjects for his own choreography. For *Revizor* ('The Government
Inspector'), he turned to Nikolai Gogol's satire on officialdom. For *Knight in a Tiger's Skin*, he
developed the themes of the twelfth-century epic poem by the Georgian Chota Rustaveli in which good
overcomes evil, and love and brotherhood are the lasting forces. The theme is old but the choreography
contemporary—symmetrical and acrobatic *pas de quatres* moulded to the music of Machavariani.
Adopting the French choreographer Maurice Béjart's emphasis on male dancers en masse, Vinogradov's *Potemkin* depicts the rebellion on board the battleship just before the Russian Revolution.
The work gives plenty of scope for the company to show its physical strength.

Two well-known Soviet choreographers have created works for the Kirov. Boris Eifman, director of
the Leningrad Contemporary Ballet company, has produced *Adagio*, a flowing piece with sculptured
movements performed to the music of Tomaso Albinoni. Dmitri Bryantsev, director of the Stanislavsky

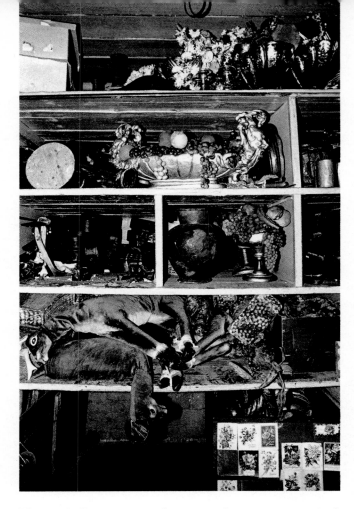

The Kirov's props room in the Maryinsky Theatre.

Theatre ballet company, has created a snappy, comic duet, popular with western audiences, called *Pas de Deux in the Style of the '30s*.

Vinogradov has encouraged foreign choreographers to bring new works and techniques into the Kirov. In recent years Roland Petit and Maurice Béjart have offered new challenges. Béjart depicts scenes from Hindu mythology in *Bakhti*, evoking angular Indian dance movements, while in *Our Faust*, to Bach's B minor Mass, and Webern's *Opus 5*, he offers the classically trained Kirov dancers works demanding athletic control, high extensions and more contoured poses. Elsa Marianne von Rosen from the Royal Danish Ballet has reset Bournonville's *La Sylphide*; the French choreographer Pierre Lacotte has staged old ballets of Taglioni, Coralli and Saint-Léon; Suzanne Farrell from the New York City Ballet visited Leningrad at the end of 1988 to set Balanchine's *Scotch Symphony* and *Theme and Variations*. The Hungarian choreographer Antol Fodor created a rock ballet, *Proba* ('The Rehearsal'), to the music of Bach and the electronic sounds of the composer Gabor Presser.

Vinogradov claims that he wants to see the Kirov company represent different companies and different eras; yet he is very aware of its position as preserver of the past. He recognizes the importance of retaining the historic works as a living museum—not reworking them with contemporary vocabulary but restoring them as closely as possible to the originals. At the same time he is fortunate in having on hand a group of leading dancers who not only dance the classics supremely well, but who are prepared through their remarkable training to adapt to modern works.

The Bolshoi Ballet in Moscow has been directed for the past 25 years by Yuri Nikolaievich Grigoro-vich. Born in Leningrad, he trained at the Vaganova School and was a pupil of Lopukhov, whose innovative choreography greatly influenced him. He joined the Kirov Ballet in 1946 as a demi-character dancer and soon began to create ballets of his own. His *Stone Flower* (1957) and *Legend of Love* (1961) proved so successful with Kirov audiences that they were later taken into the Bolshoi repertoire.

In 1964, Grigorovich left Leningrad for Moscow to become the Bolshoi's chief choreographer and artistic director. He stepped into a company brimming with talent and he has developed it. He was the right man in the right place at the right time, and he produced some of the greatest moments in the Bolshoi's history. His company of the 1970s contained an impressive list of stars: Maya Plisetskaya, Raisa Struchkova, Nina Timofeyeva, Natalia Bessmertnova, Vladimir Vasiliev, Ekaterina Maximova, Maris Liepa, Mikhail Lavrovsky.

Grigorovich is a short, sharp man with crew-cut hair and an impish grin, who maintains that his first love was the circus (many of his family were circus performers). While preserving a certain purity of line, he has shaped his troupe of young dancers into a unique, often flamboyant, style. His is a male-orientated company with the emphasis on athleticism and outsized action. Grigorovich has guarded the style and direction of the company from the influences of outsiders over a quarter of a century—something of an achievement these days when many ballet companies tend to develop homogeneously, absorbing the same cultural influences from an ever-shrinking world.

Grigorovich's supporters applaud his flashy style, his epic-sized productions that engulf the whole stage, his scenes full of swarming, leaping hordes, the steel-strong ballerinas, the intimate, lyrical *pas de deux* and the flat-out pace of his bravura choreography. His critics decry his streamlining of the classics and a lack of subtlety in his own works—all his ballets, they say, are basically the same in steps and story and lack much original choreography. His very personal seal on the company gives the Bolshoi its uniqueness—but it also restricts exciting contemporary development in other directions.

While Grigorovich's works and certain of the classics remain the backbone of the Bolshoi repertoire, there has been little effort to find other first-rate choreographers. In fact, isolation from the outside world has clipped the wings of balletic creativity throughout the Soviet Union: at the 1988 All-Union Choreographic Competitions held in Moscow, no gold medal at all was awarded, only lesser prizes. Contact with western trends up to now has been minimal. Even those Soviets who have access to the latest in western dance development—through tours, videos, or associations—have not succeeded in producing interesting, lasting works.

So far, the only western choreographer invited by Grigorovich to the Bolshoi has been France's Roland Petit, who re-created his 29-year-old ballet *Cyrano de Bergerac* for the 1988 season. The openness now reaching out to the West may produce more foreign exchanges and thus aid the Soviets in establishing contemporary styles of their own.

Like the Kirov, the Bolshoi has retained its Russian traditions by the direct, continuous handing down of ballet lore from generation to generation. For 250 years dancers have studied the same technicalities, performed many of the same repertoires and projected the same nuances, nurtured by earlier exponents. This transmission from dancer-teacher to pupil ensures the survival of the aristocratic family line of Russian classicism. The stars of the 1980s are being taught by the ballerinas and *danseurs nobles* of the 1950s and 1960s, who in turn learned their lessons from earlier performers. In today's Bolshoi Company, Nina Semizorova and Alla Mikhailchenko are pupils of Galina Ulanova. Alexei Fadeyechev is coached by his father Nikolai; Nina Ananiashvili by Raisa Struchkova; Ludmilla Semenyaka by Marina Semyonova. At the Kirov, Yelena Pankova is coached by Irina Kolpakova; Faroukh Ruzimatov by Gennady Selyutsky; Altynai Asylmuratova by Olga Moiseyeva; Veronika Ivanova and Irina Chistyakova by Ninel Kurgapkina.

The links with the past are unbroken. But how, and where, are they forged? The process begins with the young, at ballet school. In Leningrad, for instance, pupils at the Vaganova School tread the same boards as Pavlova and Nijinsky before them. In Moscow the Bolshoi School building is modern but the traditions are venerable.

The transformation from cygnet to swan, from duckling to prince, is not easy. It takes eight years of steely discipline, vision, dedication and perseverance—and there is no automatic guarantee of

(*Above*) Faroukh Ruzimatov at rehearsal in the Maryinsky
Theatre.

(*Left*) The Bolshoi at rehearsal: (*left to right*) Irek
Mukhamedov, Ludmilla Semenyaka and Yuri Posukhov
rehearse Roland Petit's CYRANO DE BERGERAC
(music: Marius Constant).

stardom at the end. Ballet legends are few and far between, but many of them have been individually nurtured at the Kirov and Bolshoi schools before taking flight into ballet history.

Entrance into these rarefied swanneries comes officially at around ten years of age. Before that, aspiring clutches of eight- and nine-year-olds take evening classes, learning musical appreciation, movement and rhythmics before taking the audition that, they hope, will change their lives.

The big moment comes every spring. In both Moscow and Leningrad, the scene is the same. At each school, more than 2,000 children try for only 90 places. With anxious parents they descend on the three-storey ferro-concrete school building on Frunzenskaya Street in Moscow or the white and yellow architectural gem on Rossi Street, formerly Theatre Street, in Leningrad. Stripped to their *trusi* (underpants), they are put through a rigorous three-part examination. Pulled and stretched like chewing-gum, they are scrutinized by a table of examiners to see whether they are physically attractive, supple and flexible. Seven hundred pass to the next stage at each school. Doctors check them to ensure not only that they are fit and healthy but to judge, as far as is possible, whether they might in the future become over-muscular, over-tall, or fat. Then their musicality is tested; they are given dance sequences and are graded on their ability to remember them. Finally, 45 girls and 45 boys are selected by each school.

(*Above*) Second-year pupils (aged about eleven) at the
Vaganova School.

(*Left*) Daily class, at the Vaganova as in most ballet
schools throughout the world, begins with *pliés*.

The Soviet state lavishes care and money on the prize pupils. It spends about 20,000 roubles on training each one over the full course of eight years. The total state subsidy for the Vaganova School alone, which has 500 pupils and 300 teachers, is 1,500,000 roubles a year.

Both the Leningrad and the Moscow Schools are self-contained institutes. The children are schooled not only in classical ballet technique but in academic studies: literature, physics, mathematics, French (the language of ballet), chemistry and the histories of theatre and ballet. Every child learns musical appreciation to help in understanding phrasing and intonation, as interpreting music is one of the most important aspects of dance. Children also study the piano, often performing for friends at informal in-house concerts where all students dance regularly in front of each other. The pupils are encouraged to take an interest in all the arts, with regular visits to museums, galleries and concerts.

In the doctor's quarters are examining rooms, a sick bay, electrical and heat-treatment apparatus for sprained ankles or tired muscles, therapy and massage tables and a dental clinic. Special equipment helps to train the body, when necessary, to conform to the unnatural positions ballet demands—stretching the muscles, perfecting the 'turn-out' from the hips, arching the foot.

The Moscow School, constructed around an open grassy courtyard, has 20 modern, airy studios, all with sloping wooden floors and large ceiling-to-floor windows. Leningrad's Vaganova School is a constant reminder of the past, its structure unchanged except for a small lift that clanks past wide twisting staircases. It has a rabbit-warren of corridors that lead to studios with high windows; the most famous is the wrought-iron-balconied room where a portrait of Agrippina Vaganova looks down. In all the studios in both schools, battered watering-cans stand in a corner. Whenever a floor becomes slippery, a pupil walks backward across it, a can held high in both hands, shaking from it a trail of musty damp. The tradition continues in the rehearsal studios of the Kirov and Bolshoi theatres themselves.

Each class has about 16 pupils who stand at three wall barres in front of a full-sized mirror. Boys and girls are segregated for daily classical class but mixed for character dancing, acting and, of course, *pas de deux* work. Tiny swans-to-be meet pint-sized potential princes for classes of polonaises and quadrilles. The boys wear black shorts and white vests, socks and canvas shoes, while their partners, hair in neat buns, wear white sleeveless leotards and gauze skirts held gracefully with the tips of the fingers as tradition requires.

The beginnings may seem slow. Many lessons in patience are to be learned as work continues on the five basic positions, the angle of incline of the head, the demands of a ram-rod back and the co-ordination of arm and foot. At times deportment is emphasized by practising in the tiny gap between barre and wall. In the second year, pink toe-shoes are tried on and first lessons are carefully and gently begun. Each succeeding year builds up strength, grace and stamina, coupled with more patience and discipline. Leningrad pupils take an active part in many of the Kirov's productions. They, and pupils in Moscow, put on complete ballets themselves during the year.

(*Opposite*) The senior class of the Vaganova School rehearsing Chopiniana for their graduation performance at the Maryinsky Theatre.

(*Overleaf, left*) A moment of reflection for Ella Karimova.

(*Overleaf, right*) In the same student, the results of the Vaganova School's intense, careful training reveal a supple body, high extensions and a strong back.

(*Above*) Between classes, schoolwork continues as usual.

(*Opposite*) Konstantin Sergeyev, Director of the school, rehearses the senior boys.

The children are by no means wholly the products of regimented conformity. In the corridors, they become normal children again—girls giggling and the boys jostling and teasing. Bags are tossed aside as an arabesque or a turn is suddenly executed on a carpeted floor. The atmosphere is relaxed. The children are outgoing to visitors, greeting them with big smiles and curtseys or bows. Then it is straight back to chatter.

Some of the students are offspring of dancers in the companies, but they still have to prove their talents on their own. One little girl in the Moscow ballet school does have good contacts, though—her grandfather is Mikhail Gorbachev.

(*Above*) At the Vaganova School graduation performance, a young soloist, Ariuna Nerovsamuchiyk, experiences a moment of anxiety before going on stage.

(*Opposite*) The Vaganova All-Russia Competition: the girls' variations, performed before the jury, with families, friends and classmates looking on.

Many of the children come from Soviet republics. Some are from Eastern Europe, and one or two are from the West. They live on the school premises. During the short breaks in the school year, they are taken to the schools' own holiday camps. In Moscow, a *dacha* in the woods at Serebryanny Bor, twenty minutes' drive from the centre of the city, offers cross-country skiing or tobogganing in winter—but not skating because it develops the wrong muscles—and swimming in the Moskva river in summer. In Leningrad, there is a *dom odikha*—literally, a House of Rest.

As the years pass, pupils who do not make the grade are regularly weeded out. The climax for the survivors comes each May when the senior students, now graceful swans and handsome princes, face examining-boards headed by the directors of each school. At the same time, directors of the Kirov and Bolshoi companies make their selections of the very best pupils. On average, about 10–12 dancers make it into the Kirov, about 6–10 into the Bolshoi. The remainder go to other companies around the country.

Natalia Dudinskaya, Artistic Director of the Vaganova, teaching her graduation class: (*left to right*) Sneyana Perkovich, Tania Alpidovskaya, Nastia Dunetz, Lena Bayenova.

Once in a company, life continues for the next 20 years in the same familiar pattern. Each day there is a daily class—usually two hours long with special exercises that start with gentle pliés and footwork and gradually build strength in the whole leg. The discipline of attending regularly and upholding standards is imperative—there is always someone else waiting in the wings. There are also endless rehearsals, and, for leading dancers, coaching by famous forerunners.

Backstage in both theatres, mazes of winding passages lead to dressing-rooms shared with opera singers; to rehearsal studios; to a canteen where dancers, musicians, stage-hands and office workers all come together; to racks of hanging costumes; to shelves of props; to massage rooms and saunas; to basic food shops which ease the daily ordeal of Soviet shopping.

Before performances, the famous raked wooden stages are vacuumed and then brushed with whisk brooms to make certain that no grit remains. An army of specialists stands by: make-up artists, hairdressers, wig-makers, costume-fitters who sew the ballerinas into their tutus at every performance, doctors who wait at the side of the stage to massage aching muscles and mop brows with tissues. Glasses of water are ready to refresh dancers after strenuous sequences. The opportunity to perform is the object of all those long years in the school studios and classrooms, forming the newest links in a long chain of classical beauty, discipline and art.

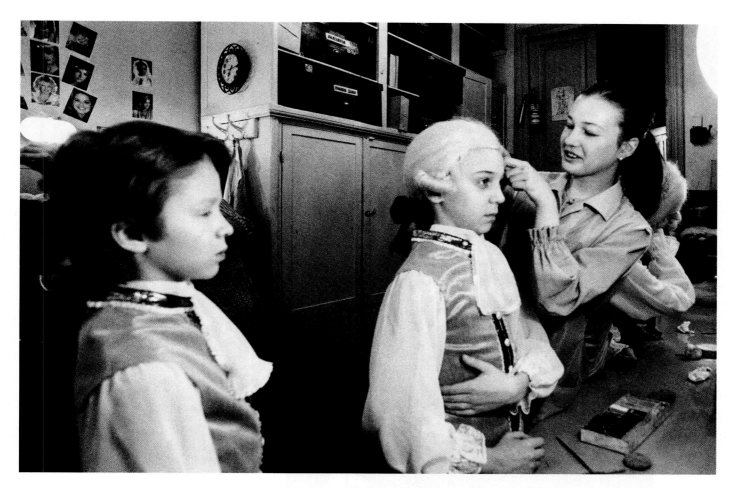

Boys being made up for the graduation performance at the Maryinsky Theatre.

There are 19 state ballet schools around the Soviet Union, including those in Leningrad and Moscow. Yet only a few of the graduates are accepted into the Kirov and Bolshoi companies. Where do the other dancers go?

Some of the most talented are to be found in the 23-year-old Moscow Classical Ballet, a company which takes full-length classical productions and new trends in choreography to cities and towns around the USSR and abroad. The Moscow Classical Ballet has no theatre base of its own in the capital, though it has offices and rehearsal studios at the old Bolshoi School, now the headquarters for *GITIS*, the State Institute for Theatrical Arts. When it returns to Moscow for regular seasons and festivals, it usually performs at the 6,000-seat Palace of Congresses in the Kremlin or at the Tchaikovsky Hall. It is a popular troupe and has many exciting young dancers.

The company, founded in 1966 by the Soviet Ministry of Culture, was first known as 'The Youth Ballet'. Its purpose was to introduce and promote Russian classical ballet and contemporary Soviet works to new audiences. In 1968 Igor Moiseyev, internationally recognized today for his colourful folk-dance troupe, became the group's artistic director and produced a programme of concert numbers and choreographic miniatures. In 1971 under the direction of Yuri Zhdanov, once the partner of Galina Ulanova, the repertoire of the now renamed 'Classical Ballet' expanded to include one-act ballets

Backstage at the Bolshoi Theatre:
storing the tutus.

choreographed by Zhdanov himself, extracts from several Russian classics and contemporary Soviet miniature works.

In 1977, the husband and wife team Vladimir Vasiliov and Natalia Kasatkina took over the company (adding the word 'Moscow' to its title), and remain the directors today. Under their guidance, the group has been moulded into a full-size company of 70 dancers that has performed in more than 200 cities in the Soviet Union and has travelled to over 30 countries. The directors have played an important role in the formation of a contemporary Soviet ballet repertoire; their own ballets form the backbone of the Moscow Classical Ballet Company.

Both were members of the Bolshoi Company for 20 years—Kasatkina one of its finest character soloists and Vasiliov a strong character dancer. They began to choreograph in the 1960s for the Bolshoi: *Vanina Vanini*, Stendhal's story to music by a young Moscow Conservatoire graduate, Nicolai Karetnikov; and *The Heroic Poem* (or *The Geologists* as it was also known), again with Karetnikov's music, about city geologists trapped by fire in the *taiga* (forest). Both ballets were well received but it was their *Le Sacre du Printemps* ('*The Rite of Spring*'), the first production in Russia, which was premiered at the Bolshoi in 1965 with Kasatkina dancing as the Possessed, that established them as a powerful creative force. Its composer, Stravinsky, declared that their production of *Rite* was the best and most Russian he had seen.

Kasatkina and Vasiliov originally choreographed *The Creation of the World* in 1971, and it is perhaps their best-known work in the West. Revived in 1978 for the Moscow Classical Ballet's repertoire, the production presents a humorous, child-like look at the Adam and Eve story: God leaps around in a night-shirt; blonde curly-haired angels wiggle their fingers; a twirling-tailed Devil with red-and-black-legged cohorts tempts with a huge globe-like apple. There are several beautiful passages, especially the *pas de deux* between Adam and Eve, where the choreographers show sensitivity in interpreting in dance form the qualities of wonderment and innocence; but the ballet is long and repetitive and often relies on cuteness to keep it alive.

In a version of *Romeo and Juliet* which stays close to Shakespeare's text, Kasatkina and Vasiliov emphasize the inevitability of the lovers' deaths by interpolating symbolic omens of doom such as leering carnival masks and skeletons. *Mischiefs of Terpsichore* is a thinly woven story about a ballet competition and the pomp and ceremony surrounding it. It is really an excuse to show what the company does best: tossing off showy concert numbers with panache.

The repertoire also includes the full-length romantic ballet *Natalie, or the Swiss Milk-maid*, staged by Pierre Lacotte of France in 1980. *Divertissement* programmes demonstrate the different styles and abilities of the members of the Company—Petipa's *Carnival in Venice*, Bournonville's *Flower Festival at Genzano*, Asafiev's *Flames of Paris*, Petipa's *Esmeralda*; and there are newer works by Estonia's Mai-Esther Murdmaa, Vietnam's Nguen Van Nam, France's Roland Petit and Maurice Béjart, and America's George Balanchine.

Maya Plisetskaya, who has danced with the Bolshoi ballet since 1943, epitomizes the ideal Soviet ballerina. To a base firmly grounded in Russian classical technique, she has added the vitality, spontaneity and passion of contemporary Soviet ballet. Early in her career, she captured the quintessential elements of her characters, taking risks and loving the challenge. Plisetskaya brought excitement to the audiences of the 1950s, 60s and 70s, who flocked to see her sharply executed and expansive movements, her high, powerful leaps, her dynamic characters full of expression and fire.

In the late 1980s she is still dancing, bringing to the stage the dramatic intensity of earlier years, although her dancing is now inevitably tempered by gentler movements.

Plisetskaya was destined to become a ballerina. She was born into a theatrical family, the daughter of a silent-screen film actress, sister of dancer Azari Plisetsky, niece of two of the Bolshoi's great dancers, Asaf and Sulamith Messerer (who taught Plisetskaya the *Dying Swan* solo when she was 14 years old) and cousin of designer Boris Messerer. On entering the Bolshoi Ballet School in 1934, Plisetskaya was taught for six years by Elizaveta Gerdt, whose father had taught Pavlova and Karsavina. Here she learned the pure academic technique and developed the lyrical qualities of the classic ballerina, although, even then, her fiery temperament often lent added expressiveness. She performed as a student in several of the Bolshoi's productions. When she graduated and joined the ranks of the Bolshoi Ballet it was as a soloist, rather than in the *corps de ballet*. In her preparation for the role of Masha in *The Nutcracker* she was fortunate to be coached and taught for three months by the great teacher Agrippina Vaganova, who inspired the young ballerina and encouraged her to bring out her own individuality.

During the next ten years, Plisetskaya made her début in both the ballerina and leading character roles. Her Raymonda was self-assured, her Odette fragile and trusting, her Odile calculating and cunning. Her Myrthe in *Giselle* was austere and commanding, her Zarema (*The Fountain of Bakhchisarai*) possessive and passionate, and her Kitri (*Don Quixote*) flirtatious and impetuous. Plisetskaya was seductive in the acrobatic dual-natured role of 'Mistress of the Copper Mountain' (in *The Stone Flower*), where suppleness and expressiveness transformed her from cool Russian beauty to slithering lizard.

When Ulanova retired from the stage in 1962, Plisetskaya became prima ballerina of the Bolshoi. Her performances sometimes met with disapproval from the purists who felt that technique, and not interpretation, should be the most vital element, yet she remained utterly compelling to watch. During the early Grigorovich years, her energy on stage generated excitement; her daring was both thrilling and surprising. She encompassed the stage in expansive steps, making intricate and difficult footwork seem easy. She flew through the air in her famous leap—a soaring *jeté* with her back foot almost touching her head.

Awarded the Lenin prize in 1964, she made many tours overseas with the Bolshoi, winning much acclaim. She married the Soviet composer Rodion Shchedrin in 1958 and the two have regularly worked together. He composed the music for the *Carmen Suite*, based on Bizet's score; and for her own choreographic works—*Anna Karenina*, *The Seagull* and *Lady with a Lap-Dog*.

Plisetskaya's portrayals often glorified sensuality, on a stage where passions have traditionally been more restrained. Her Carmen in Alberto Alonso's *Carmen Suite* oozed with sexual appeal: in her stance, the swing of her hips, the dark-eyed glances, the Latin temperament. In her own ballet, *Anna Karenina*, she vividly portrays the anguish and passion of Tolstoy's heroine, torn between her own desires and the rules of nineteenth-century society. It is a ballet filled with theatrical effect, its shattering emotions and chilling climax underlined by Shchedrin's eclectic score. Today, performing in her latest creation, *Lady with a Lap-Dog*, based on the short story by Anton Chekhov, she conveys the silent yearning and subtle sensualism of the heroine, Anna Sergeyevna, by dramatic projection rather than by dancing technique. The work has spectacularly beautiful sets, costume and lighting, yet contains little actual dance. It is made up of frozen poses for the *corps de ballet* and a series of gymnastic *pas de deux*.

Besides her artistry and interpretation, Plisetskaya will be remembered for her remarkable, undulating arms. As a swan—either in *Swan Lake* or as the *Dying Swan*, which has become her signature piece (after performing it, she invariably dances it again as an encore)—she embodies a majestic Queen of Birds, her arms quivering and rippling so fluidly that they seem to be without bones.

Offstage, the red-headed Plisetskaya is intense and often outspoken, ready to do battle for her art. She makes no secret of her rift with the Bolshoi's director, Yuri Grigorovich. She feels he is too conservative and not open enough to outside ideas. For the past 16 years she has not been included on his Bolshoi tours abroad. However, this has not stopped her career. She is always in demand: to dance, to teach, to coach, to travel. She was director of the Rome Opera Ballet, 1984–85, and of Spain's national ballet company in Madrid in 1987. She still has many supporters in Moscow and is able to perform her own works at the Bolshoi Theatre, usually when the main bulk of the company is off on tour.

Plisetskaya has had long associations with Roland Petit and Maurice Béjart. In 1973 Petit created for her his soulful ballet *Rose Malade* which she premiered in Marseilles. In 1975 in Moscow she performed the lead in Béjart's *Bolero*—a strenuous role usually taken by a man. Bolshoi audiences were enthusiastic. In 1976, she danced another Béjart work, *Isadora*, based on the life of the American dancer Isadora Duncan. Plisetskaya toured the United States with Béjart's company in 1977. First with the Rome Opera Ballet, then supported by the Ballet Théâtre Français de Nancy, she performed Serge Lifar's *Phèdre* in 1985, a one-act tragedy based on the Greek legend of the queen who falls in love with her stepson Hippolytus, and, on being rejected, engineers his death. It provides an opportunity for Plisetskaya to project conflicting emotions in an interpretation that is forceful, yet never excessive. She vividly conveys the desperation of a character pulled apart by passions she cannot control.

(*Opposite*) The student dancers look on from the wings at the graduation performance.

The Waltz *pas de deux* from CHOPINIANA with Irina Yelonkina and Igor Markov: a view from the wings of the Vaganova graduation performance.

Maya Plisetskaya is one of the great dancers of our time, not because she is the most lyrical or the most disciplined, but because she took the fundamentals of her fine training, with skill and acumen perfected them, built on them, and gave full rein to her natural flair for the dramatic.

Vladimir Vasiliev is a versatile master of his art. His Prince in *Sleeping Beauty* is romantic and noble; his Basil (*Don Quixote*) fun-loving and quick-witted; as the sad Mejnun (*Leili and Mejnun*), he propels his passion to the point of exhaustion; as the flirtatious and heartless Pulcinella he makes his hands and body speak for his masked face; as Macbeth, he shows courageous energy and ambitious fear; as the seedy and pitiful Professor Raät (*The Blue Angel*), he grovels for attention. His best known role, Spartacus, was branded with a strength, passion and tenderness not duplicated since.

Vladimir Vasiliev has been recognized as one of the great—if not the greatest—male dancers of our time. His beautiful clear technique and rare sensitivity combine with an actor's ability to give credence to his roles. 'I have never seen the likes of Vladimir Vasiliev!' said Kasyan Goleizovsky, the innovative Soviet choreographer in whose ballets Vasiliev danced in the 1960s. 'He is a real genius of the dance.' Goleizovsky spoke of how the dancer 'always works at full steam', and how 'he grasps every situation, works on it and finds a solution of his own'.

Vasiliev is not dependent on mime for characterization but conveys character through movement. He has a magnetic presence on stage, and an inborn feeling for the subtleties of his roles, searching for psychological meanings. He is a reliable and gallant partner, sensitive to his ballerina's needs. His talent has won admirers and many awards around the world. In recent years he has branched out into choreography and films, both with distinction.

Along with Maya Plisetskaya, Vasiliev has done more to promote his country's ballet outside its borders over the past twenty years than any other Soviet dancer. (Nureyev, Baryshnikov and Makarova have become part of the western dance world; Vasiliev and Plisetskaya remain Soviet citizens, anchored to their homeland, always returning to it.)

Individually the two dancers have travelled far and wide, performing at galas as guest artists, teaching classes, serving on juries, choreographing, assuming the role of director to foreign companies. Above all, they have demonstrated in their own superlative dancing the complementing duality of the old Russian and the newer Soviet styles. Both artists are exacting yet exciting, precise yet daring, tender yet passionate, lyrical yet heroically strong.

Vasiliev entered the Moscow Choreographic School at the age of nine. The son of a Moscow workman, his natural aptitude for dancing was quickly noted and he was given much attention.

In his first year, he partnered a tiny, thin-limbed girl with big brown eyes in the school concert. They performed a polonaise together—'really more of a walk', she was to admit in later years. This pupil was Ekaterina Maximova, subsequently to become one of the Bolshoi's most renowned and most beloved ballerinas and Vasiliev's constant partner. They were married in 1961 and today travel the world together in a unique balletic partnership. A recent example came in January 1988 in Paris, when they were guests with the Kirov Ballet, on its winter tour at the Palais des Congrès. They gave two memorable performances of *Giselle*, mature in interpretation yet youthful in presentation. Vasiliev's Albrecht was a man who, besotted by the beautiful young girl, truly forgot his noble birth and official betrothal. His happiness blinded him to the terrible deception he was living. When circumstances forced him to realize it, he was shattered. As he watched Giselle re-live their moments together in the 'mad scene', Vasiliev's acting of Albrecht's grief and suffering was genuinely moving. Maximova's Giselle, enriched with the finest traditions of the Russian school, was poetic in its grace and beauty.

Vasiliev has performed almost all the classical roles with virtuosity and seemingly inexhaustible strength. He has had success with contemporary works, beginning with the creations of Goleizovsky. In recent years Vasiliev has worked with Roland Petit and Maurice Béjart, creating the leading role in the latter's *Petrushka*.

As a choreographer, Vasiliev's first work was the ballet *Icarus*, premiered at the Bolshoi Theatre in 1971. It was followed by the beautiful plotless ballet, *These Charming Sounds*, created to the music of Mozart, Corelli and Rameau, which evoked the style of western choreographers such as Balanchine. In his full-length ballet *Macbeth*, created in 1979, Vasiliev demonstrated his facility for welding colourful drama to exciting choreography. Freely translating Shakespeare's tragedy, the ballet showed thoughtful and original touches. Athletic and powerful male dancing created vivid battle scenes and the three witches were danced by men, who, swathed in sepulchral rags, spun furiously on pointe like ballerinas. The ballet was a great success with audiences.

Yet, at home in Moscow, Vasiliev has fallen from official Bolshoi favour. The artistic director, Yuri Grigorovich, has been pruning his company into a more youthful shape—and disagreements have surfaced with older members. In 1979 Vasiliev, along with Plisetskaya, Maximova, Mikhail Lavrovsky and Maris Liepa, resisted Grigorovich's decision to remove epics such as Leonid Lavrovsky's *Romeo and Juliet* from the repertoire and to restage them himself.

As the rift widened, Vasiliev danced less at the Bolshoi, and turned to other pursuits: choreographing, and producing ballets for television and for the cinema. He also toured regularly abroad. When in Moscow he and Maximova continue to take daily class at the Bolshoi with the revered teacher Asaf Messerer and they still occasionally perform there. Vasiliev's ballet *Anuita* (from the story *Anna round the Neck* by Chekhov) is now in the Bolshoi repertoire and he and Maximova dance the leading roles. Vasiliev has set *Anuita* for the ballet company at the Teatro de San Carlo in Naples and the Riga (Latvia) Company which he brought on tour to Paris in 1988.

As this book in a sense closes a door on the past, another door in the shape of Mikhail Gorbachev's *glasnost* is opening. How it will continue to affect the arts—both Soviet and western, and especially the ballet world—is not yet clear. Will the closeknit community of Russian dance expand to include more outside influences? Will its insular companies become more like most international ones and welcome foreigners into them? Will there continue to be bigger and better exchanges of Soviet and western stars on a regular basis? Will more exposure to modern technique affect the pristine quality of the Russian school? Will the political and ideological content of new ballet scenarios grow less?

As the Kirov and Bolshoi make more and more frequent visits abroad, will enthusiasm for them wane? Will they produce enough fresh choreography to satisfy western tastes?

The decade covered by the photographs in this book has been an important and interesting era of the Russian Ballet.

Another awaits.

MAYA PLISETSKAYA

Maya Plisetskaya combines the finest traditions of the Russian classical heritage with Soviet bravura and brilliant acting. She excels as the *Dying Swan*, a role that is now associated with her as much as it was with Anna Pavlova. The piece is short, hardly a showcase for Plisetskaya's pyrotechnics—indeed, the steps, a series of *bourrées*, are not difficult in themselves. It is how the tragedy is interpreted that makes it a challenging role. Plisetskaya chooses to depict it as a struggle to survive, rather than acceptance of death. Her magnificent creature fights for its life, proud rather than fearful. Eloquently she conveys this battle for survival with her whole body—the regal carriage, the fluid lines of her long, wing-like arms that beat and flap in protest, the anguish in her face.

Phèdre, a very different work, provides equally broad scope for Plisetskaya's dramatic abilities.

(*Above*) Plisetskaya in the Ballet de Nancy's production of PHÈDRE (choreography by Serge Lifar/music by Georges Auric)

(*Opposite*) Plisetskaya in PASSAGE OF LIFE, created for her in Paris in 1986 (Astad Deboo/Philip Glass)

(*Pages 44–45*) Plisetskaya as the Dying Swan

(*Opposite*) Plisetskaya in Phèdre

(*Above and overleaf, left and right*) Plisetskaya in The Dying Swan (Fokine/Saint-Saëns)

THE KIROV BALLET
OF LENINGRAD

The mantle of the Russian Ballet heritage falls on the shoulders of today's Kirov Company, whose present dancers perform on the same wooden stage where Pavlova, Nijinsky and Karsavina once danced. Treasuring and preserving the classic heirlooms of the past, yet reaching out for the new, today's Kirov dancers interpret both equally well: *La Bayadère* and *Bhakti*; *Le Corsaire* and *Potemkin*; *Swan Lake* and *Knight in a Tiger's Skin*.

The company's prima ballerina has been dancing for nearly forty years. She is Irina Kolpakova, once taught by Agrippina Vaganova. Today she acts as coach to aspiring ballerinas, though she is still to be seen on stage, expressing the special brand of Kirov lyricism. In *Papillon*, supported by Sergei Berezhnoi, she flits like the butterfly of the title with gossamer lightness. In *Chopiniana* (*Les Sylphides*), she is a will-o-the-wisp, the essence of the romantic ballerina.

Yelena Yevteyeva, another of the senior ballerinas, shows off her classic lines with legato phrasing. More angular yet full of expressive quality is Galina Mezentseva, whose movements are always well placed and strong. Olga Chenchikova, a graduate of the Perm ballet school, is fluid and controlled in classical roles, while in contemporary works, such as *Our Faust* and *Knight in a Tiger's Skin*, she displays a well-coordinated technique. Tatiana Terekhova is a splendid technician with a pure line and high elevation, attacking the choreography with bravura.

A band of rising stars show that lessons are being learned well. Yelena Pankova has a quality of freshness and liveliness; Zhanna Ayupova is an innocent and fragile-looking ballerina who offers softness and neatness in such roles as *Chopiniana*. Yulia Makhalina dances with assurance and character detail; Veronika Ivanova, pert, pretty and one of the youngest, performs with grace and charm—an ideal *Giselle*, as seen when she danced the ballet with Alexander Lunev on the Company's 1988/9 tour to Paris, where also the Bolshoi stars Vladimir Vasiliev and Ekaterina Maximova, as guests, offered a deeper, more mature interpretation of the same roles.

Konstantin Zaklinsky leads the male dancers, with a style that is both elegant and reliable. Yevgeny Neff is a handsome dancer and a good partner in classical roles although his finely-tuned body seems more at ease in athletic contemporary works. Young Alexander Lunev has good potential; he is a dancer of refined technique with effortless leaps and powerful beats. Marat Daukayev is reliable and strong; the tall Makarbak Vaziev has a high extension and careful partnering.

But it is the partnership of the flamboyant Faroukh Ruzimatov and the beautiful, willowy Altynai Asylmuratova which has stirred the most ex-

Faroukh Ruzimatov in Act I of GISELLE (Perrot, Coralli, Petipa, Slonimsky, rev. Vinogradov/music, Adam)

(*Pages 52–53*) Alexander Lunev and Veronika Ivanova in Act I of GISELLE

citement. Ruzimatov's full-blooded performances exude energy and force; he demonstrates remarkable control in leaps and in corkscrew turns, and possesses astonishing elevation. Asylmuratova has immaculate technique and great musicality; her expressive and interpretive abilities are greater than almost any other current ballerina's. Together on stage Ruzimatov and Asylmuratova create an electrifying partnership that continues to develop. They were the first Soviet dancers permitted by the Kirov to appear as guests with the American Ballet Theater company in New York in 1988, and with the Royal Ballet in London in 1989; partly as a result of this, they have now gained superstar status.

There is no finer *corps de ballet* in the world than the Kirov's. Its precision and grace are widely praised. In *Giselle* and *La Bayadère*, as indeed in other classical works, the ballerinas move as one: lines impeccably straight; arms, legs and action of the heads all synchronized; movements precisely drilled yet flowing. There is a sense of unity and purpose, yet they never lose their feminine grace.

GISELLE, Act I: Altynai Asylmuratova and Faroukh Ruzimatov

GISELLE, Act I: Ekaterina Maximova and Vladimir Vasiliev, guest artists from the Bolshoi; (*below*) Ekaterina Maximova

GISELLE, Act I: Ekaterina Maximova in the 'Mad Scene'

GISELLE, Act II: Hilarion (Dimitri Korneyev) and the Wilis

(*Above*) GISELLE, Act II: Maximova and Vasiliev

(*Opposite, above and below*) Altynai Asylmuratova and Faroukh Ruzimatov in
GISELLE, Act II

(*Overleaf*) The *corps de ballet* in Act II

SWAN LAKE, the 1895 St Petersburg production in 3 acts (Ivanov, Petipa, Sergeyev/
Tchaikovsky). Act I Sc. II (*below*): Irina Chistyakova; (*right*) Yevgeny Neff and
Tatiana Terekhova
(*Overleaf*) The first scene of Act I

SWAN LAKE, Act I Sc. II: (*above*) Asylmuratova and Ruzimatov; (*opposite*) the *corps de ballet*

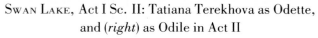

SWAN LAKE, Act I Sc. II: Tatiana Terekhova as Odette,
and (*right*) as Odile in Act II

(*Overleaf*) Terekhova and Neff in the Act I Sc. II *pas de deux*

(*Pages 74–75*) Terekhova and Neff in the Act II *pas de deux*

LA SYLPHIDE (Bournonville, Von Rosen/H. Lövenskjold): (*below*) Svetlana Efremova
and Vladimir Petrunin

LA SYLPHIDE: (*opposite above*) Lyubov Galinskaya as Effie, with Ravil Bogutinov;
(*opposite below*) Nikolai Kovmir as the witch Madge

La Sylphide: (*above*) the *corps de ballet*; (*opposite*) Svetlana Efremova; (*overleaf*) the
corps de ballet, with Natalia Pavlova (*left*), Tatiana Rusanova (*centre, on floor*) and
Irina Sitnikova (*right*)

CHOPINIANA [LES SYLPHIDES] (Fokine/Chopin): (*above and below*) Olga Likhovskaya in the Prelude; (*opposite*) the *corps de ballet*

CHOPINIANA: (*opposite*) Irina Chistyakova in the Prelude; (*above*) Zhanna Ayupova in
the Mazurka; (*below*) Irina Kolpakova and Sergei Berezhnoi in the Waltz *pas de deux*

CHOPINIANA: Yelena Pankova and Yevgeny Neff in the Nocturne *pas de deux*
(*above*); (*opposite*) Neff with the *corps de ballet*

LE CORSAIRE (Petipa, Gussev/Adam, Pugni et al.): (*opposite*) Eldar Aliev as Konrad
and Olga Chenchikova as Medora; (*above*) Alexander Lunev as Ali; (*overleaf*)
Chenchikova and the *corps de ballet* in the 'Jardin Animé' scene

Le Corsaire: (*above*, *left to right*) the three Odalisques, Veronika Ivanova, Zhanna Ayupova, Ella Kamalova; (*opposite*) Irina Chistyakova as Gulnare

LE CORSAIRE: (*overleaf left*) Konrad, Eldar Aliev, Medora, Olga Chenchikova and
(*on floor*) Ali, Alexander Lunev; (*overleaf right*) Chenchikova as Medora in Act I;
(*pages 96–97*) the 'Jardin Animé': Chenchikova and the *corps de ballet*

(*Pages 98–99*) Paquita (Petipa/Minkus): Act III. Yulia Makhalina and Sergei
Berezhnoi in the *Grand Pas*

Paquita: (*above*) Alexander Lunev; (*opposite*) Tatiana Terekhova

PAQUITA: Galina Mezentseva (*above*); Yelena Kamalova and Natalia Pavlova (*left and right*, *below*); (*opposite*) Chenchikova

PAQUITA: (*above*) Olga Chenchikova and Marat Daukayev; (*opposite*) Veronika
Ivanova

PAQUITA: Yulia Makhalina and Alexander Lunev; (*opposite*) Altynai Asylmuratova

La Bayadère (Petipa/Minkus): Act III, The Kingdom of the Shades, Konstantin
Zaklinsky and Yelena Yevteyeva (*above and opposite*)

(*Overleaf*) The entrance of the *corps de ballet* at the beginning of Act III

LA BAYADÈRE, Act III: (*opposite*) Zaklinsky and Yevteyeva; (*above*) Tatiana
Terekhova and Marat Daukayev

(*Pages 114–115; above and opposite*) OPUS 5 (Béjart/Webern): Olga Chenchikova
and Marat Daukayev

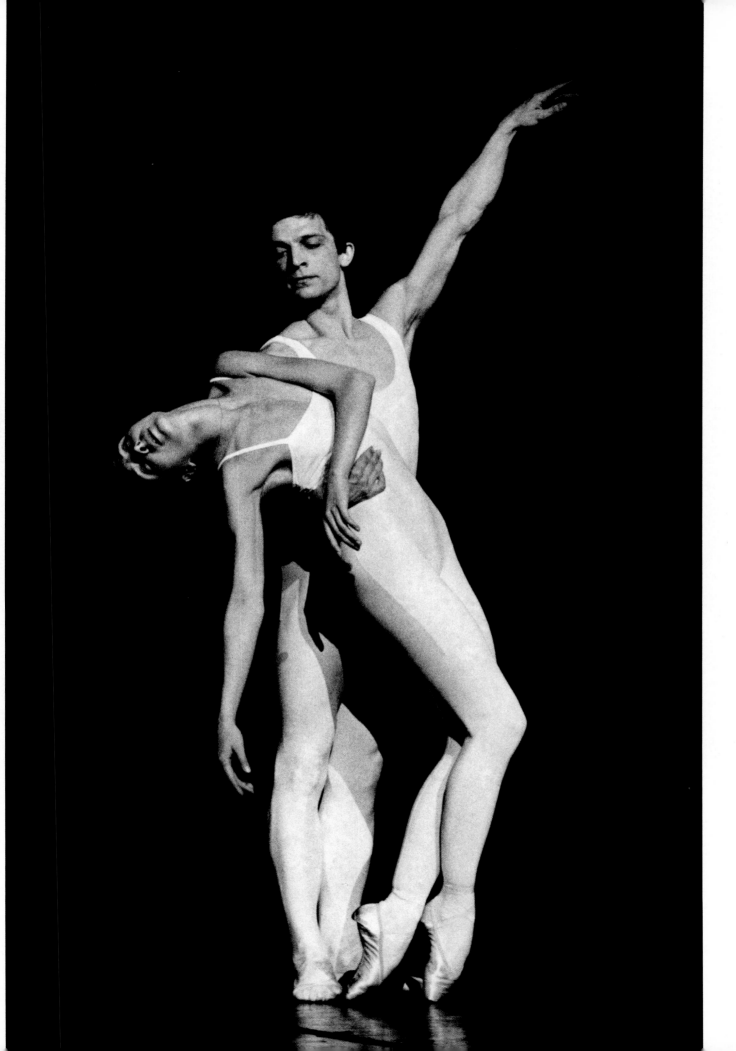

ADAGIO (Boris Eifman/Albinoni): Yevgeny Neff (*above and opposite*)

Our Faust (Béjart/Bach): (*opposite, above, below and overleaf*) Olga Chenchikova
and Yevgeny Neff

KNIGHT IN A TIGER'S SKIN (Vinogradov/Machavariani):
(*above*) Olga Chenchikova (*left*) and Tatiana Ariskina
with Ruzimatov and Aliev behind;
(*right*) Faroukh Ruzimatov

KNIGHT IN A TIGER'S SKIN: (*above, left to right*) Yevgeny Neff, Tatiana Ariskina, Olga Chenchikova, Faroukh Ruzimatov; (*below, left to right*) Neff, Chenchikova, Ariskina, Aliev

KNIGHT IN A TIGER'S SKIN: Tatiana Ariskina and Faroukh Ruzimatov

(*Above*) Bhakti (Béjart): Altynai Asylmuratova and Faroukh Ruzimatov

(*Opposite*) Knight in a Tiger's Skin: Faroukh Ruzimatov

(*Above*) PAPILLON (Maria Taglioni/Jacques Offenbach, 1860): Olga Likhovskaya and
Andrei Bossov

(*Opposite*) CARNIVAL IN VENICE (Petipa/Pugni): Svetlana Efremova and Valeri Emetz

(*Overleaf*) ESMERALDA (Petipa/Adam et al.): the *pas de Diane* with (*left to right*)
Irina Pankova, Tatiana Ariskina, Tatiana Gumba

POTEMKIN (Vinogradov/A. Tchaikovsky): (*above*) the first scene; (*below*) Death
(Gennadi Bababin) and his victim (Unga Kamalova)

Revizor (Vinogradov/A. Tchaikovsky): Vadim Guliayev

REVIZOR: (*above*) the company, with Nikolai Kovmir (*centre*) as the Governor,
Natalia Bolshakova as his daughter and Ninel Kurgapkina as the Mother; (*below*)
Valeri Emetz as the Postman and Nikolai Kovmir (*centre*) as the Governor; (*opposite*)
Vadim Guliayev as the Government Inspector, Khlestakov, with Natalia Bolshakova

THE MOSCOW
CLASSICAL BALLET

The Moscow Classical Ballet is a small, travelling company with a large number of talented dancers. Several of them—Isayev, Shliapina, Paly, Gorbatsevich, Terentiev, Trofimchuk and, more recently, Stepanenko and Malakov—have been top prize-winners at the international ballet competitions of Moscow and Varna, Bulgaria. In 1981 Irek Mukhamedov, then a company member, won the Grand Prix medal in Moscow, before going on to join the Bolshoi and become its superstar.

The leading man for several years has been the quiet, boyish Stanislav Isayev, a gold medallist at Varna and winner of the French Nijinsky prize. He is a refined performer with a high extension, agility and soft, accurately placed landings, as shown in his role of Adam in *The Creation of the World*. Here his sense of humour and his timing are displayed and the development from child-like innocence to adult temptation is clearly characterized. As Romeo, he is romantic and lyrical. Isayev has been fortunate to partner in both these ballets the great Bolshoi ballerina, Ekaterina Maximova, who often performs as a guest with the Moscow Classical Ballet. She brings her experience, her exquisite technique and her great interpretive gifts.

Alexander Gorbatsevich is a noble, more traditional dancer with a pure style, while Igor Terentiev demonstrates the neat and polished footwork characteristic of the Danish Bournonville school. The leading ballerina is Galina Shliapina, a dancer of lyricism and sensitivity. Tatiana Paly is a technician who delights in boldly tossing off *fouettés*—often quadruples—with an insouciant, graceful air.

To Russian audiences, the Moscow Classical Ballet presents a pleasant change from the perennial diet of period classics; it offers a range of fresh and lively productions and the opportunity to see talented dancers in favourite old selections as well as contemporary works by Soviet and foreign choreographers.

(Pages 140–141 and opposite) Ekaterina Maximova, guest artist from the Bolshoi, and Stanislav Isayev in a *pas de deux* from ROMEO AND JULIET (Kasatkina, Vasiliov/ Prokofiev)

ROMEO AND JULIET: (*above, left to right*) Alexander Gorbatsevich, Stanislav Isayev and Nina Osipian as Mercutio, Romeo and Benvolio; (*below*) Isayev with maskers at the Verona carnival

ROMEO AND JULIET: (*above*) Ekaterina Maximova as Juliet with Svetlana
Shakhotkina as her mother; (*below*) Shakhotkina as Lady Capulet, with attendant
ladies, on hearing of Juliet's 'death'

(*Right*) THE CREATION OF THE WORLD (Kasatkina, Vasiliov/A. Petrov): Isayev and Maximova as Adam and Eve

(*Overleaf left*) FLOWER FESTIVAL AT GENZANO (Bournonville/E. Helsted): Tatiana Paly and Igor Terentiev

(*Page 149 and left*) La Bayadère (V. Chabukiani/Minkus): Galina Shliapina and Alexander Gorbatsevich

THE MISCHIEFS OF TERPSICHORE (Kasatkina, Vasiliov/J. Strauss et al.): (*below*) the company; (*opposite above*) Natalia Shalachnova; (*opposite below*) Stanislav Isayev

THE BALLET SCHOOL: HOMAGE TO ULANOVA (Vasiliev/various composers): (*left to right*) Vladimir Vasiliev; Alla Mikhailchenko and Viktor Barikin; Irina Piatkina and Andris Liepa; Nina Semizorova and Alexei Fadeyechev

In the triple role of dancer, choreographer and director, Vladimir Vasiliev brought a small group of dancers to the Théâtre des Champs-Élysées in Paris in the summer of 1983. The programme, *Stars of the Bolshoi*, which he devised and directed, introduced young Bolshoi soloists to European audiences and demonstrated three facets of a dancer's life: the daily ritual of class, its progression to the performance of concert pieces and, finally, expansion into the contemporary style. The programme also clearly showed how the Bolshoi's past is linked to both the present and the future by the handing down of traditions. The group in Paris—ten dancers, one student and a ballet-mistress—bound together four generations of dancers on stage in a delightful evening of dance.

The ballet-mistress here was the great Galina Ulanova, the coach for many years of Vasiliev and two ballerinas of exceptional technique, Ekaterina Maximova and Nina Timofeyeva. These three experienced dancers mingled on the Paris stage with the stars-in-the-making: Nina Semizorova, Alla Mikhailchenko, Irina Piatkina, Valery Anisimov, Viktor Barikin, Alexei Fadeyechev and Andris Liepa, who in turn demonstrated what they were learning to young Nadia Timofeyeva. The ten-year-old student, just starting her ballet life, watched wide-eyed as first Vasiliev, then the others, performed the structured exercises of the 'classroom ballet', which Vasiliev dedicated to Ulanova.

In the final part of the programme, *Fragments of a Biography*, created by Vasiliev after a visit to Argentina, the classically-trained dancers appeared in a different light—the women, now pert and frisky, were dressed in short fringed skirts while their men slouched, black fedoras low over their eyes, watching them with that particularly Latin sexual predatoriness. Soon all the dancers were swaying and bending to the rhythms of the tango. Vasiliev, as the older man, joined the young dancers, re-living his past, both consoled and tormented by visions of his unattainable love—danced by Maximova, who floated in and out of the smoke in a long white dress. As he strutted about, thumbs poked into waistcoat pockets or playing nonchalantly with his black hat, Vasiliev offered fresh and unexpected views of his great artistry: a master craftsman at work.

(*Opposite*) THE BALLET SCHOOL: Andris Liepa

THE BALLET SCHOOL: (*above*) Maximova and Vasiliev (*centre*), with Piatkina and
Liepa (*left*), Mikhailchenko and Barikin (*right*); (*opposite*) Andris Liepa

COPPÉLIA, *pas de deux*: (*above and opposite*) Andris Liepa and Irina Piatkina

FRAGMENTS OF A BIOGRAPHY (Vasiliev/Cedron, Falu, Piazzolla, Torres, Yupanqui):
(*above*) Andris Liepa and Alla Mikhailchenko; (*opposite*) Vasiliev and
Mikhailchenko

(*Above*) Nina Semizorova as Kitri in an excerpt from Petipa's DON QUIXOTE

(*Opposite*) FRAGMENTS OF A BIOGRAPHY: Nina Semizorova and Alexei Fadeyechev

THE BOLSHOI BALLET
OF MOSCOW

The Bolshoi Ballet company is aptly named: the word means 'big', and the company is big in every respect. It boasts 300 dancers and 400 backstage workers; it presents spectacular productions, with choreography that requires broad, sweeping movements; and it demands a special brand of streamlined dancer to fill the stage—heroic, powerful men and technically assured, vivacious ballerinas.

The company is fuelled by the energies of Yuri Grigorovich, whose hand, like that of the statue of Apollo driving the chariot on the portico of the columned Bolshoi Theatre, firmly holds the reins of the Moscow branch of the Russian balletic tradition. His repertoire represents the rich Russian heritage and draws on the colour and soulfulness of the national character. Historical classics are more showily performed than in Leningrad, and more theatrically staged. His own productions, using the music of Soviet composers, create a style in which the emphasis is on dance rather than mimed drama and the spotlight tends to fall on the male dancer.

His *Spartacus*, created in 1968, has become one of the best-known Soviet ballets. A surging mass of male dancers fills the stage as the slaves struggle against Roman oppression. The production was a showcase for the outstanding artists of that period—the virtuosity of Vladimir Vasiliev as Spartacus; Maris Liepa's brilliant portrayal of the cruel, calculating Crassus; Natalia Bessmertnova's passionate and tragic Phrygia; Nina Timofeyeva's sensual and voluptuous Aegina. Today the leading role belongs to the young Tatar Irek Mukhamedov, who blazes his way across the stage, eyes smouldering, a fiercely rebellious force. He continues his fight against evil in Grigorovich's *Golden Age*, set in the 1920s, in which, dressed in white, he catapults after the bad guys. In such classics as *Giselle* and *Raymonda*, Mukhamedov slows down and shows his schooling in a noble bearing and classical form.

Other male dancers might lack his force, but offer other qualities: Alexei Fadeyechev, son of Plisetskaya's partner Nikolai, is a dignified and elegant dancer; Yuri Vasuchenko has a gentle style and steady partnering; Alexander Vetrov generates powerful drama in the role of Abderachman in *Raymonda*; Andris Liepa follows his father Maris's *grand jeté* leaps with his own more lyrical style. With the graceful and sensitive young Georgian ballerina Nina Ananiashvili—his partner since school days—Liepa was a guest with the New York City Ballet in 1988. Later he danced with the American Ballet Theater for a year.

Grigorovich's ballerinas are equally at home interpreting spirited contemporary roles and the gentler styles of the classics: Natalia Bessmertnova, a senior dancer of world-wide renown, one of the greatest Giselles ever; Ludmilla Semenyaka, whose Kirov training is now spiced with Bolshoi bravura and crisp attack; Nina Semizorova, with her sharply defined dramatic technique; Alla Mikhailchenko, who displays unaffected purity; and Nina Ananiashvili.

THE GOLDEN AGE (Grigorovich/Shostakovich): (*pages 166–167*) the *corps de ballet*; (*right*) Natalia Bessmertnova as Rita

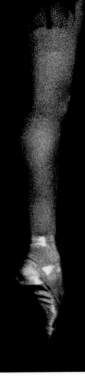

THE GOLDEN AGE: (*left*) Andris Liepa as Boris and Ludmilla
Semenyaka as Rita

THE GOLDEN AGE: (*opposite*) Ludmilla Semenyaka; (*above*) Irek
Mukhamedov; (*below*) Mukhamedov and Bessmertnova

THE GOLDEN AGE: (*opposite above*) Ludmilla Semenyaka; (*above and opposite below*)
Semenyaka and Andris Liepa

GISELLE (Perrot, Petipa rev. Grigorovich/Adam): (*above*) Maria Bulova in the
'Peasant' *pas de deux* from Act I; (*right*) Natalia Bessmertnova and Yuri Vasuchenko
in Act I

(*Overleaf*) GISELLE, Act I: the friends of Giselle

GISELLE: Act I, with (*opposite above*) Bessmertnova and Vasuchenko; (*opposite below*) Bessmertnova in the 'Mad Scene'; (*above*) the death of Giselle (Bessmertnova, with Vasuchenko)

GISELLE: Alla Mikhailchenko in Act I

GISELLE: the 'Peasant' *pas de deux* in Act I with Maria Bulova and Vladimir Liakhin

GISELLE, Act II: The Queen of the
Wilis (Ilze Liepa) and Hilarion
(Mikhail Gabovich)

RAYMONDA (Petipa, Grigorovich/Glazunov): Ludmilla Semenyaka in the title role
and Irek Mukhamedov as Jean de Brienne
(*Opposite*) Alexander Vetrov as Abderachman

RAYMONDA: (*above*) Semenyaka with Alexei Fadeyechev and Yuri Posukhov;
(*opposite*) Semenyaka and Mukhamedov

(*Overleaf*) Semenyaka with Alexander Vetrov; (*right*) Tatiana Bessmertnova and
Posukhov

RAYMONDA: *(below and opposite)* Semenyaka and Mukhamedov

RAYMONDA: (*above*) Semenyaka; (*opposite above*) Vetrov; (*opposite below*) the
Hungarian *divertissement* from Act III

Spartacus (Grigorovich/Khachaturian): (*above*) Nina Timofeyeva as Aegina;
(*opposite*) Natalia Bessmertnova as Phrygia

(*Overleaf left*) Timofeyeva as Aegina; (*overleaf right*) Bessmertnova (Phrygia) with
Vladimir Vasiliev as Spartacus

SPARTACUS: (*opposite*, *above and below*) Nina Timofeyeva (Aegina) with the late
Maris Liepa as Crassus; (*above*) Vasiliev and Bessmertnova as Spartacus and
Phrygia

SPARTACUS: (*above*) Vasiliev in the title role; (*opposite*) Maris Liepa as Crassus

(*Right*) Spartacus (Vasiliev) rallies his
army of slaves

(*Overleaf*) The last moments of
SPARTACUS: Vasiliev as the rebel
leader is put to death by the Romans

Acknowledgements

I would like to express my gratitude to the following, without whose support and assistance this volume could not have been realized: my parents, the families Kasem-Beg, von Schweder, Brui and Pechatnikov; Sophie Julien, Marina Kuznetsova and Elena Bespalova; the intrepid Calmann and King team of Laurence King, Elisabeth Ingles, Paula Iley, Marianne Calmann and Judy Rasmussen; U. Bär Verlag's Ulrich Bär; Ernst Halter; the Public Relations Department of Kodak-Pathé; the Cité Internationale des Arts; Irène Commeau of the Échanges Internationaux Éducatifs et Culturels; UNESCO; the press attachés of the Lincoln Center for the Performing Arts, the Espace Pierre Cardin, the Théâtre Municipal de Paris, the Palais des Congrès, the Théâtre National de l'Odéon, the Spectacles ALAP, the Spectacles Lambroso, particularly Nicole Gonzalez, Danielle Cornille, Albert Sarfati and Suzi Lefort; the administrative personnel of the Kirov Opera and Ballet Theatre, particularly Oleg Vinogradov and Maxim Krastin; the administrative personnel of the Bolshoi Theatre, particularly Yuri Grigorovich and Stanislas Lushen; the staff of the Moscow Classical Ballet; the staff of the Vaganova Choreographic School, particularly Natalia Dudinskaya, Konstantin Sergeyev, Leonid Nadirov and Marina Vivienne; the USSR Ministry of Culture; the USSR Commission for UNESCO, with special thanks to Sergei Klokov for his invaluable help with this project in the Soviet Union; and, not least, my fellow contributor to the project, Margaret Willis, not only for her introduction but for help on many details. Finally I wish to express my deepest gratitude and admiration for all the artists, performers, choreographers, composers, teachers, stage and support personnel that make the Russian ballet tours such a universal success.

The black and white photographs for this book were printed by Anne-Marie Filaire of the Yvon Le Marlec Laboratoire in Paris.

ALEXANDER ORLOFF

I would also like to add my thanks to those of Alexander Orloff, particularly to the Directors and the dancers of the Kirov, the Bolshoi and the Moscow Classical Ballet companies; to Maya Plisetskaya; Vladimir Vasiliev; the editors of *Sovyetski Balyet* magazine; the Entertainment Corporation of London; and Elisabeth Ingles.

MARGARET E. WILLIS

Index

Page numbers in *italic* refer to illustrations

———— 208 ————